IMAGES
of England

PENN AND
BLAKENHALL

St Bartholomew's church, Penn, as it appeared in the 1930s. There has been Christian worship on the site since about 1025, and parts of the present church date from the thirteenth century although most of it was built after a major reconstruction in 1764–5.

St Luke's church in Upper Villiers Street, Blakenhall, with St Luke's school in the foreground. Built unusually in ornate brickwork, the church was consecrated in 1860.

IMAGES
of England

PENN AND BLAKENHALL

Compiled by
Alec Brew

TEMPUS

First published 1998
Copyright © Alec Brew, 1998

Tempus Publishing Limited
The Mill, Brimscombe Port,
Stroud, Gloucestershire, GL5 2QG

ISBN 0 7524 1527 1

Typesetting and origination by
Tempus Publishing Limited
Printed in Great Britain by
Midway Clark Printing, Wiltshire

Penn and Blakenhall is Alec Brew's fourth book in the *Archive Photographs*
Series, chronicling Wolverhampton in a century of photographs.

Already published are:
Codsall and Claregate
Tettenhall and Pattingham
Willenhall to Horseley Fields

Also compiled by Alec Brew in The *Archive Photographs* Series are:
Albrighton and Shifnal
Staffordshire and Black Country Airfields.

In preparation:
Ettingshall and Monmore Green
Heath Town and Fallings Park
Bushbury and Featherstone

Contents

The heart of Blakenhall, around 1926, with Upper Villiers Street running to the centre top, by St Luke's on the left and Marston Road separating the allotments at the bottom from Villiers Engineering. The much larger Sunbeam factory fills most of the picture.

St Phillip's church, Penn Fields, which was built for the growing population in the area in 1859, as Wolverhampton expanded along Lea Road. The war memorial is on the left.

Introduction

The area of Wolverhampton which has come to be known overall as Penn has been completely transformed over the years of this century. Before the First World War it was a series of tiny rural villages, Bradmore, Finchfield, Castlecroft and Penn itself, housing a farming community which had more connection with other local farming communities than with the western suburbs of the industrial towns of Wolverhampton, Blakenhall and Graiseley.

One of the major institutions in the area, the Royal School, was built as the orphan asylum, to house the orphans of the victims of the 1854 cholera epidemic, on a field which had been a cholera camp. Of necessity this was well outside the town and, even by the turn of the century, it was still possible to walk from Pearson Street in Blakenhall across nothing but cornfields, behind the orphanage and all the way to Penn church.

The expansion of Wolverhampton had already begun, but the building of closely packed terraced houses was limited mostly to Lea Road, on the other side of the Penn Road. Blakenhall was noted as a centre for tinware manufacturing and japanning, that is the enamelling of tinplate products and their rich decoration. Many large factories were engaged in the trade including Richard Stroud's Niphon Works, and John Marston's Jeddo Works. The skills of the trade led many tinplate manufacturers naturally into bicycle manufacture.

It is said that before 1900, where there were only half a dozen bicycle manufacturers in the towns of Nottingham or Leicester, there were thirty in Wolverhampton and it was inevitable that many of these would turn their attention to powered vehicles, motorbikes and cars.

Blakenhall was a typical inner town suburb of terraced houses packed tightly around factories, schools and churches, but what set it aside from many such suburbs was the nature of the industry which came to dominate the area. If Detroit is Motown USA, it is Wolverhampton, and in particular the suburb of Blakenhall, which was once Motown UK, an unofficial title later appropriated by Coventry. The skilled workmen of the Blakenhall/Graiseley area made Sunbeam Cars, John Marston's Sunbeam motorcycles, AJS motorcycles, Star, Briton, Stuart and Starling Cars and Clyno cars and motorcycles. They also made Diamond, Orbit, Wulfruna and Wolf motorcycles, Turner cars and Villiers engines; the area thus gave a home to an incredible galaxy of famous names, with many smaller manufacturers also operating there.

At 'knocking off' time thousands of workers poured from these factories to walk to their terraced homes. However, with the expansion of Wolverhampton's public transport routes, by tram and then trolleybus, new suburbs could spring up, firstly down Lea Road to Penn Fields and then across the whole area, engulfing farm after farm.

After the First World War new private and municipal housing spread outwards until it included Penn and then reached the natural barrier of Penn Common, on which housing could not be built. Penn's compensation was that the whole area often tends to be called Penn, so that the Penn cinema was actually in Warstones, and Penn Halt, on the railway, was nowhere near Penn village.

These days, life in the Penn and Blakenhall area is less momentous than it used to be, the likes of Malcolm Campbell or Henry Seagrave no longer come along to view their land speed record breaking cars being built. People along the Penn Road no longer catch glimpses of the latest AJS, Sunbeam and Clyno motorcycles being taken on a road test. The area does not reverberate to the sounds of the country's most powerful aero-engines being tested. The area is quieter and less exciting, but no less pleasant for that.

The Wearwell Cycle Company's factory being built in Great Brickkiln Street, Graiseley. Wold motorcycles were also built here.

One

Penn

A thousand years ago the parish of Over Penn, as it was then known, was owned by Lady Godiva's son, Alfgar, and in the churchyard of St Bartholomew's is the base of a preaching cross which dates from that time, the first church being built around 1200. The village is thus an old one, a small farming community scattered down the hill from the church to the important Wolverhampton to Worcester/Kidderminster road, known for its first section as the Penn Road. Slowly Penn's large neighbour, Wolverhampton, expanded down this road until now Penn church stand on the very edge of the town, and therefore the whole Black Country/Birmingham conurbation. It still has, however, the magnificent views of the rural landscape of south Staffordshire and Shropshire.

The gardeners at Penn Hall laying drains under the front lawn before the First World War. Fourth from the left is Jack Whitlock, and one of the maids by the door was his wife.

COUNTY OF STAFFORD,

Upper Penn, Lower Penn, and Wombourne.

IMPORTANT AND VERY VALUABLE

FREEHOLD

Residential Property

Known as

"PENN HALL,"

VALUABLE FARMS, SMALL HOLDINGS,

ACCOMMODATION & BUILDING LANDS

Fully-Licensed Public House,

GRAVEL MINES, COTTAGES, GARDENS

Admirably situated in the Parishes of Upper and Lower Penn, and of Wombourne, and all Mines and Minerals thereunder. The whole forming the Estate of the late JOHN PERSHOUSE, Esq., and covering an area of

388a. 0r. 25½p.,

To be submitted for Sale by Public Auction, by

MESSRS. NOCK & JOSELAND

At the

"Star and Garter Hotel," Wolverhampton,

On

WEDNESDAY, THE 6th DAY OF DECEMBER, 1899,

At Four o'clock in the Afternoon, punctually.

Particulars and Plans may be obtained from Messrs. COBBETT, WHEELER, & COBBETT, Solicitors, 61, Brown Street, Manchester; Mr. W. E. ANSLOW, Es , Office, Wombourne, Wolverhampton; Mr. J. H. MAYBURY, Surveyor, 25, Booth Street, M ter; Messrs. BUTCHER, LITTON, & POWNALL, Chartered Accountants, 42, Spring Gardens, Manchester; or of the Auctioneers, Messrs. NOCK & JOSELAND, 48, Queen Street, Wolverhampton; and Bank Buildings, Kidderminster.

JOHN STEEN & CO., PRINTERS, OLD GRAMMAR SCHOOL WORKS, ST. JOHN STREET, WOLVERHAMPTON.

Penn Hall had been leased for forty years by William Underhill, a wealthy ironmonger, but when he died in 1899, the Persehouse family who owned the property sold it off.

Pupils and three of the teachers at St Bartholomew's school, Penn, c. 1890. On the front row, fifth from the left, is Tommy Whitlock, son of the Penn Hall gardener.

Penn Manor Farm on Church Hill, c. 1910. They are, from left to right: Fred Chidlow, Nora May Chidlow, Samuel Ambrose Madeley (a local shire horse dealer). The tree is a Tettenhall Dick pear and they used to sell the pears, which were only edible after cooking, for 1d a packet.

Haymaking in Manor Road Fields, which were opposite the Fox and Goose. The man on the rear seat of the mower is Walter Turner, who later farmed at Compton. The man on the horse is Sam Madeley.

Fred Chidlow harrowing in Church Fields, around 1910. The last horse did not leave Manor Farm until 1950 when the last tenant, Reg Massie, bought a Ferguson tractor.

An attractive group of cottages on the Penn Road opposite the Hollybush Inn before the First World War. They were known variously as Penn Hall cottages and Hollybush cottages.

A pair of cottages on the Penn Road which includes the premises of T.J. Nash, a taxicab owner, *c.* 1910. They were located between Stubbs Road and Coalway Road.

The St Catherine's convalescent home for women and children, in the area of St Catherine's Crescent, around 1910. It was founded in 1873 by Harriet Sparrow and enlarged in 1889 to house eighteen beds.

The Beeches on the Penn Road in 1938, when the Royal Hospital moved the convalescent home to this larger site. It still stands in front of the Penn Hospital.

The Rose and Crown on the Penn Road when it was the terminus for the horse-drawn bus service from Wolverhampton. On the right is Samuel Tharme's three-horse bus, with the conductor standing alongside. On the left is the dogcart from Penn convalescent home.

The Avenue as it appeared before the First World War, with the wall of the Beeches on the left. The walls on each side of this narrow lane still remain.

Penn cricket club's 1st XI at the opening of the Muchall Road ground in 1908. On the back row, from left to right: J. Steventon (umpire), D. Hickman, W. Boon, A. Herbertson, H. Whittle, J. Hickman, D. Crutchley, W. Rogers, H. Higgs, C. Causer (umpire). On the front row: Revd Addenbrooke Holden (president) H.A. Page, H.D. Stratton, F.W. Page.

An impressive way to travel to an away match, Penn cricket club on the way to Enville on Whit Monday, 1908. The party included: J. Baugh, Mrs Crowther, H. Higgs, C. Hodgkiss, G. Ryall, Mrs Ryall, W. Rogers, V. Robinson, H. Roden, F. Taylor, H. Woodward.

Straw Hall on the Penn Road stood near to the orphanage and was later demolished when the road was widened. There is a story that one owner of Straw Hall was murdered and his body thrown in a sand pit opposite.

Three children strolling together up Goldthorn Hill, around 1910.

St Bartholomew's church, Penn, before 1911. To the right of the church is the stone base of a Saxon cross, which is usually called Lady Godiva's Cross, as she is known to have owned parts of Penn.

A Victorian house in Wakeley Hill, Penn, with Lydia Whitlock in the doorway before the First World War.

Muchall Manor Farm, Penn, when it was sold as part of the Lloyd estate in 1901.

Penn Road at the junction with Manor Road before the First World War. These buildings are all now gone, to make for the dual carriageway section of road.

The post office on the Penn Road, as it appeared in the 1930s, with the sun-blind pulled out.

A section of the Penn Road during the First World War. These houses still exist on the north side near the orphanage.

The Avenue, as it neared the top of Goldthorn Hill when it was just a country lane through a rural area in 1906.

Vicarage Road in Penn between the wars.

The artisan's section of Penn golf club having a dinner in the Rose and Crown in the 1920s.

The brother of Percy Stallard (who was a famous local bicycle racer) on his Sunbeam Model 9 in Penn, *c.* 1931. He was a local bus driver and used to go grass track racing on this bike.

A Model 'T' Ford taxi operated by Herbert William 'Bill' Boulton at his first garage in Penn on the corner of Church Hill. He probably bought a Ford as he had the contract to refuel Model 'T' chassis which were being driven from Trafford Park to the coach builders.

Bill Boulton's subsequent garage at the bottom of Lloyd Hill. The sign which says 'Boulton's Garage' was made from the rudder of a First World War fighter.

Penn cricket club's 1st XI in 1932. On the back row, from left to right: N.P. Lee, E.R. Whitehouse, W. Moseley (chairman), J.L. Cartlidge, W.L. Dann, K. Hill. On the front row: B.W. Whitehouse, H.T. Mason, C.E. Kirkham (captain), F.S. Bowles, R.J. Whitehouse.

The entire student body of Miss Corker's private school in Windhurst Road, Penn, *c.* 1933. On the back row, first from the left, is Ken Peplow.

Miss Stroud ran another local private school, around 1928, which was on the Penn Road near the end of Coalway Road, where the shops are now. On the back row, second from the left is Roy Sidebotham and then Tom and Ted Jenks. Second left on the middle row is Ken Peplow.

Manor Farm, Penn, with Ken Peplow on the horse, around 1936. He was one of a number of people who used to go riding from there.

Penn home guard platoon, date unknown, probably in the grounds of Penn Hall.

The Vintage motor cycle club spring trial outside the Park Hall Hotel in 1953. They are, from left to right: G.S. Davidson (a winner of the TT in the 1920s on a Levis), Mr Pullin and his father Cyril Pullin, (a winner of the TT in 1914 on a Rudge-multi). The bike is a Pullin-Groome, amazingly, from 1920.

The Penn bowling club, in 1945, which was sited in Manor Road. George Edwards is standing on the extreme left; he was the groundsman of the club, and the gardener at Muchall Hall.

Country dancing at St Bartholomew's school, Penn, in March 1955.

The rear of Muchall Hall, which was sold and demolished in 1961. The price realized for the Hall and its six acres of land was £16,500.

Penn cricket club 1st XI, *Express and Star* trophy winners in 1957. On the back row, from left to right: Geoff Dorke, Gordon Lord, Cyril Underwood, Graham Soden, Paul Brimley, Eddie Pearson, John Peplow, Fred Emson (umpire). On the front row: John Underwood, Trevor Welsh, Ian Butler (captain), Vernon Crowe, Teddy Page, Margaret Higgs (scorer).

No. 141 Mount Road, a pleasant cottage in Penn during the early 1950s. It was sold with Muchall Hall and has since been demolished; a row of new houses is now being constructed on the site.

The boys' rounders team at Penn school in the early 1950s. The teacher is Patrick Gregory.

A class group at St Bartholomew's in the 1950s.

A group of Penn school infants during the 1950s. This is one of my favourite pictures in the book; it is pleasant to see a class group in such an informal setting.

The garden of No. 305 Penn Road, which shows Manor Road school behind. Manor Road closed and was demolished when Colton Hills was opened in 1976. The school had united with Graiseley secondary school and the Municipal grammar school which operated at first on three sites while Colton Hills was built.

A section of the school photograph at Penn secondary school, Manor Road, taken in March 1960. The headteacher in the centre is W. Graham.

St Bartholomew's school teachers, *c.* 1975. They are, from left to right: Doreen Russell, Cerys Griffiths, Kathleen Blakemore, Irene Turner, Helen Deane, Mike Pallowe. On the front row: Kate Wearing, Stella Packham, John Allbutt (headteacher), Kay Vasey, Mary Bednarski.

A class group in the playground at St Bartholomew's school, with the church in the background, *c.* 1968.

A later class group at St Bartholomew's school, 1971/2.

The No. 11 trolleybus to Penn, in this case a Sunbeam F4, made in Blakenhall, with a Park Royal body.

The girl's netball team at St Bartholomew's school, Penn, in 1980.

The shops on the Penn Road at the junction with Coalway Road, in the 1950s, looking remarkably quiet. In the 1960s the Penn Road was described as the most congested suburban road in the country.

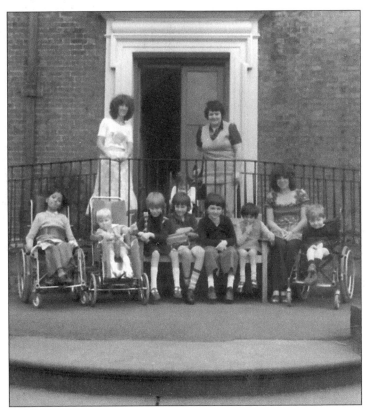

The door of Penn Hall in 1977. It became a special school in 1974, having been used as a nurses' home and then a police residential home since being sold out of private ownership in 1947. A comparison with the first picture in this section shows that everything about the door is the same, except for the ramps built for the wheelchairs.

Two

Penn Common

Penn Common has long been the playground of the people to the west of Wolverhampton. There used to be a racecourse on part of it and in the same area the members of Penn golf club came to an agreement with the Commoners to create their golf course. The common is also a favourite area for riding and walking and its very existence created an effective barrier to the further expansion of Wolverhampton's suburbs, which has meant that the common has remained in Staffordshire while the village became part of the borough of Wolverhampton.

Some of the members of Penn golf club, shown outside the clubhouse, not long after the club won the right to play on Penn Common in 1892. They are, from left to right, (left hand group): C. Elwell, Mrs N. Mander, N. Mander. On the back row of the central group: J. Hill, E. Hickman, Miss Earl, T.W. Lovatt. Seated (central group): R. Bailey, Mrs A. Owen, Lady Mander behind Wentworth Walker, R. Smith and standing in front of the post, R. Lewis. On the right of the picture: J. Mitchell Hill, L. Wilkie.

Brook Cottage on Penn Common, sometime before 1905. The brook is named Lloyd Brook and was one of the boundaries of the land granted to Lady Wulfruna in 994.

A pond on Penn Common, probably that in front of the Turf Tavern and the Turf Cottages.

The Penn golf club clubhouse as it first appeared, built next to the Barley Mow pub, which is no longer in this use. The golfers played in the area which had previously been a racecourse.

Five AJS testers on one of their motorcycles, probably on Penn Common. They used to take the bikes on a test run from Blakenhall down the Penn Road to Penn Common and further on to Enville Common.

Tom Whitlock, a Sunbeam car tester on Penn Common, in a car fitted with makeshift bodywork for road testing purposes.

A golfer arriving at the clubhouse in his Sunbeam sedan during the 1930s.

Male members of Penn golf club outside the clubhouse in 1934.

The GPO football team on the pitch on Penn Common which they used in 1950. On the front row, second from the left is Percy Kyte.

The lady members of Penn golf club, around 1965.

Members of St Bartholomew's youth club on Penn Common in 1952. They are, from left to right: Pam Healey, Janice Martin, Rosemary Pritchards, -?-, -?-, Clare Cartwright, Jane Eyre, Christine Brittell, -?-, -?-, -?-, Jack Cartwirght (on shoulder), Pete Murray, and the boy in the front is Nigel Millwall.

Three
Penn Fields and Warstones

Penn Fields was the first part of the rural area to the west of Wolverhampton to be urbanized as housing spread along Lea Road, and by the middle of the last century it had become sufficiently populous to become a parish in its own right, with the building of St Phillip's church. New municipal housing was built on the Beckminster and Birches Barn estates after the First World War, followed by the huge Warstones estate in the 1930s.

Looking down Church Road towards St Phillip's church, which was built in 1859 on land given by W.H. Sparrow of Penn Court, to cater for the growing population.

Frederick William Keay and his wife Mary Ann (née Perks) with three of their seven children who are, from left to right: Fred, Lily, Fanny. Fred Keay farmed Coalway Farm at the turn of the century and had a famous business cultivating Arran Pilot potatoes.

Six of the Keay children outside Coalway Farm, c. 1904. They are, from left to right: Gertie, Mary, Lily, Maud, Eddie, Fanny.

Penn Fields hockey club, *c.* 1899. They played on a pitch in Coalway Lane.

"KYBER PASS"
LEA ROAD 1895

In the middle of the last century Lea Road was a tiny lane leading only to Lea Farm. Housing spread along the lane and in 1895 only this constriction known as 'The Khyber Pass' remained. The houses on the left were demolished when the road was widened.

Though Wolverhampton's tram system was already in being, the service to Penn Fields was opened with these Wolseley motor buses. This one is setting off for Penn Fields in 1904.

A Wolseley bus arriving at Stubbs Road in 1907. The bus service continued until the tramlines had been laid in 1909.

A Lorain system tram entering Lea Road from the Penn Road, around 1909. The wall of Pennhurst is on the right, and St Peter's church is in the distance.

Stubbs Road, Penn Fields, with the tramlines running up to the Penn Road, *c.* 1911.

Penn Fields football club, 1910/11.

Graseley Old Hall, at the end of Carlton Road is the oldest house in Wolverhampton, usually dated to 1485; it is shown here in 1913. Recently bought by the actress Susan Williams (stage name Susanna Pope), it is open to the public on the last Sunday of every month.

The War Memorial opposite St Phillips church, Penn Fields. One of the thirty-nine names recorded from the First World War is Douglas Morris, who has another memorial in St Peter's churchyard. They commemorate his bravery, in continuing to use his wireless aboard his sinking ship.

George Hill, a tobacco merchant with premises in Broad Street, and his brand new Star 14/30 hp in 1925. With him are, from left to right: his children Margery, John, Alec and his wife, Hortense. They are outside the AJS social club, later called the Woodfield social club.

Lea Road after the Lorain system trams had been replaced by the overhead system in 1921.

By the late 1920s, the trams had been replaced on the Penn Fields route by trolleybuses and this one (right) is shown at the terminus in the 1930s.

A wedding at St Phillip's church, Easter 1939. In the foreground are, from left to right: -?-, Bunty Bills, -?-, -?-, Marjorie Hudson (née Kyte – the wife of Mr Hudson the butcher at Merry Hill), Mrs Stella Bills.

The Rose Queen celebration from St Chad's church, gathered in Penn Fields in 1933. On the third row, from the right, is Mary Simmonds, who remained to be Mrs Simmonds after marrying a displaced person after the war, as he took her name.

Pinford Lane in Penn, probably during the 1930s. The impressive row of trees must have been there before the houses were built.

Showell Lane in Penn. This was almost the limit of suburban expansion.

Wartime bomb damage in Carlton Road. Local legend has it that the bomber was aiming at Fischer Bearings in Blakenhall, which was a German company before the war and was therefore well known to them.

The VE Day street party in Regent Road, Penn.

The coronation day party in Rindleford Avenue, Warstones estate, which included children from Swancote Drive.

The staff of the Penn cinema in the early 1960s. Seated, from left to right: Mr Turvey (assistant projectionist), Cyril Moore (chief projectionist), Mr Minton (manager), Mrs Pape (head of sales), Mrs Minton, Mrs Violet Goodway (head cleaner).

Elaine Jenkins outside her junk and antique shop on the Lea Road/Upper Zoar Street junction in the 1950s. She was eventually forcibly evicted from the property.

A Springdale primary school class in 1953.

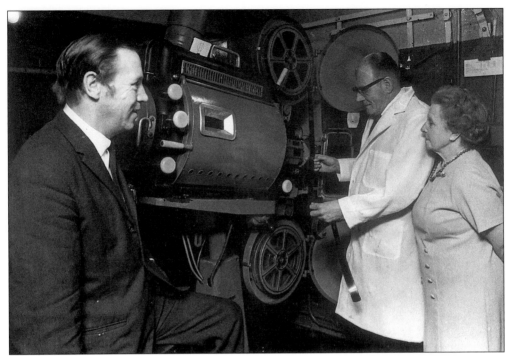

The projection room at Penn cinema just before its closure in 1973. The equipment was sent to India. They are, from left to right: Mr Crane (manager for the last seven years), Cyril Moore (projectionist for all of the cinema's thirty-six years), Mrs Violet Goodway (cleaner for thirty-four years).

The Penn cinema in the year of its closure (1973) with Cyril Moore on the roof. Built in December 1937, and one of forty-six cinemas owned by B.T. Davies, the Penn was a popular and well equipped suburban cinema. It was demolished to make way for a supermarket.

Four
Bradmore, Finchfield and Castlecroft

During the twentieth century, the three tiny rural hamlets of Bradmore, Finchfield and Castlecroft were transformed into the epitome of suburbia. The farms gave way to a large amorphous mass of housing, with little in the way of industry, and only the small beacons of Bantock Park and the Bantock House Museum being noteworthy.

Mrs Annie Bantock, in her dog cart outside the front door of Bantock House, just before the turn of the century.

A more modern form of transport owned by the Bantocks, photographed on the Chapel Ash side of West Park in 1906, with the chauffeur at the wheel.

Bradmore St Phillip's football club who played in the Church and Chapel League, 1923/4. The goalkeeper (centre) was Norman 'Nobby' Lewis and on the goalie's right is Bill Armstrong. Frank Bickerton was the captain, seated with the ball on his right leg.

Trysull Road, Bradmore.

The opening of the new bowling green at the Plough Inn, Trysull, with many members from the Bradmore and Finchfield areas.

Edward Thomas Keay, who farmed Oxbarn Farm, *c.* 1910. He is seen here with his nieces, Gertie and Fanny. There is the shadowy figure of another, unknown, man behind.

The New Inn, Finchfield, on the junction where the Chestnut Tree is now. The gentleman in the middle in front of the window with a cap is Mr Williams.

A group of local farmers outside Harper Adams College, with the agricultural students they sponsored behind, c. 1927. Among them are Fred Chidlow of Manor Farm, Penn, Ernest Chidlow of Mill Farm, Wightwick, and Walter Turner of Compton Farm.

Dan Brew, ganger in charge of the permanent way on the railway from the Tettenhall to Baggeridge Junction, which included the section through Penn Halt. He is sitting on his first motorized ganger's trolley, c. 1930.

Mrs Evelyn Kyte walking up Windmill Lane, Castlecroft, from the Mermaid, in the winter of 1941.

Mrs Kyte outside her house, the Ferns, in Windmill Lane in another bad winter, 1946/7. She is about to deliver bread from B. Woods service bakery by sledge, because the roads were impassable for her van.

The Signals Platoon of the Home Guard outside Bantock House in 1944. On the back row, seventh from the left is Bob Edwards, who had recently transferred from the Guy Motors' Home Guard. On the front row, second from the right is Captain Stanford, the CO and sat in the centre is Major Graham, one of the owners of the *Express & Star*.

The No. 32 trolleybus to Oxbarn Avenue, leaving the town terminus by the Chubb building.

The cleaning staff of Sprindale school after winning the Cleanest School Award in the late 1970s. On the back row, from left to right: Lily Harrington, Josie Miller, Margaret Parkes, Dick Denson (caretaker), Joan Harriman, Margaret ? On the front row: Vera Kendrick, Ada Collins, Eadie Jones, Mavis ?, Iris Denson.

Finchfield cricket club in 1971. Formed in the 1950s they never had their own ground and played at the time at Claregate, later moving to The Bratch. On the back row, from left to right: T. Gallagher, D. Crawshaw, A. Palmer, K. Millard, D. Watkins, C. Turner, G. Perks. On the front row: B. Dalziel, D. Coppen, P. Noakes, G. Lewis, J. Bardell, B. Fisher.

Five

Blakenhall

The name of John Marston dominates the suburb of Blakenhall, where his japanware company became Sunbeamland. This famous manufacturer of bicycles and motorbikes, with his Sunbeam Motor Car Co., owned the biggest factory in the area, building cars, buses, aircraft and aero-engines. His son, Charles, founded the Villiers Engineering Co., alongside the Sunbeam, to produce cycle components and then two-stroke engines. All the extensive buildings of these three companies still exist but they now house many different companies. Alongside the Marstons, were the Lisles, with their Star, Briton and Starling cars, and the Stevens Brothers with their AJS motorcycles, forming a concentration of automotive expertise unrivalled anywhere. Surrounding these factories and others, such as Orbit and Diamond motorcycles and Turner Cars, were the homes of the thousands of skilled workmen who produced some of the most famous products in the world, which won Grand Prix races, the Isle of Man TTs and broke land speed records.

St Luke's church in the depths of winter, before the First World War. The view is looking down Bromley Street, with St Luke's infant school to the right, and the junior and senior schools by the church.

St Luke's vicarage.

St John's church served the inner part of Blakenhall, having been completed in 1760. The far side of the fine Georgian square was demolished to make way for the first part of the ring road, which cuts off the rest of Blakenhall from the town centre.

The workforce from John Marston's cycle department at the Paul Street Works, which later became Sunbeamland, in 1888. John Marston himself is on the right holding a Sunbeam tricycle, and his son Charles on the left holding the bicycle.

The interior of Sunbeamland, with Sunbeam bicycles being assembled in 1927, much later than the previous picture. This scene would have changed little in the previous forty years.

The orphanage before the turn of the century with the chapel to the right. Opened through the efforts of John Lees (a local hardware factor) for the children of victims of the cholera outbreak of 1849, it moved from a temporary building to this site on Goldthorn Hill, the site of a former cholera camp, in 1852.

The cadet force at the rear of the Royal Orphanage, as the institution was renamed with royal approval in 1899. By this time the number of children had grown, from 13 in 1850, to 300.

Girls at the orphanage playing croquet and skipping. The spire of St Luke's is in the centre background.

The girl's dormitory in the Queen Alexandra Wing. The bell for rising was at 6.30 a.m. in winter, 6.00 a.m. in the summer, with classes from 7.30 a.m. and prayers and breakfast at 8.00 a.m. Bedtime was 8.00 p.m.

Calisthenic exercises to music for the girls.

A group of the boys at the Royal Orphanage before the First World War. They are standing in their greatly disliked smocks, the uniforms being modelled on those of the Blue Coat school in London.

Wolverhampton Wanderers with their first trophy, the Wrekin Cup, 1883/4. They began life as Blakenhall St Luke's in 1877, when the Revd Barcroft presented a ball to some of the pupils. In 1884 they were playing at a ground just off the Dudley Road, having moved from Goldthorn Hill. The manager on the right has been superimposed onto the original picture of the team.

St Luke's football team, 1906/7. By this time their offspring, the Wolves, had finally moved to the Molineux on the other side of town.

The Fountain Inn, No. 401 Dudley Road, with Martha Robinson, publican Noah Robinson and daughters Elsie, Hetty and Lizzie in 1909. There was a local saying based on the four pubs in the area – 'Why Not' 'The British Queen' wash 'The Black Boy' in 'The Fountain'.

Star and Briton cars with Edward Lisle at the wheel of the Briton, and Sir James Percy standing alongside. Lisle's Star Engineering began building cars in Frederick Street, Blakenhall, in 1896, having previously built bicycles. The Briton range was added as a cheaper alternative.

The engine shop at Star in 1910, the year they built their first aero-engine and aircraft.

The Star monoplane on display at the Olympia Aero Show in 1910. The engine and aircraft were designed by Granville Bradshaw who later became chief engineer at ABC Motors. The Star was entered for the 1910 flying meeting at Wolverhampton, but did not achieve sustained flight until modifications were made in the following year.

Upper Villiers Street, Blakenhall, in 1910. This view looks from St Luke's church showing the huge expansion of the Sunbeam Motor Car Co., since it was formed as an offshoot of John Marston Ltd in 1905.

The Sunbeam 12/16 hp, built mainly from French Berliet parts, in Upper Villiers Street, outside the Moorfield Works in 1904. This was before the car company was split from the bicycle company.

The temple-like lodge to Graiseley House, just off the Penn Road, Blakenhall; Graiseley Hill is just to the left of the lodge. Graiseley House was bought by the Stevens Brothers as the headquarters of AJS.

An artist's impression of the Niphon Works in Lower Villiers Street, originally the home of Robert Stroud and Co. Ltd, tin plate manufacturers and japaners, founded in 1868, who later made bedroom furniture. Though exaggerated in this drawing, it was nonetheless an extensive works and is mostly still there today, although occupied by a host of smaller companies.

A large family in Elm Farm Road, Blakenhall: John and Mary Jane Peplow and their thirteen children. The children's names (order unknown) were: Jack, Sam, Ernie, Bill, Walter (who ran away and joined the Navy age 14), Florence, Albert, Frank (who died on the Somme), Harold, Elsie, Eadie, Lizzie, Gladys.

The Salter family of Franchise Street, Blakenhall, before 1914. On the back row, left to right: Emily, Richard, Winifred. On the front row: Gertrude, Dolly, Agnes, -?-.

The winning Sunbeam Tourist Trophy cars photographed outside the Moorfield Works canteen in 1914.

Marston workers pouring out of Sunbeamland, date unknown. The Swan With Two Necks pub is on the right.

The 1915 wedding of Mr and Mrs Davies (née Salter) in the garden of George Gough, the builder, in Villiers Street. Mr Gough is fourth from the right in the middle row, and his daughters are the three seated (on chairs) on the left, and the one seated extreme right.

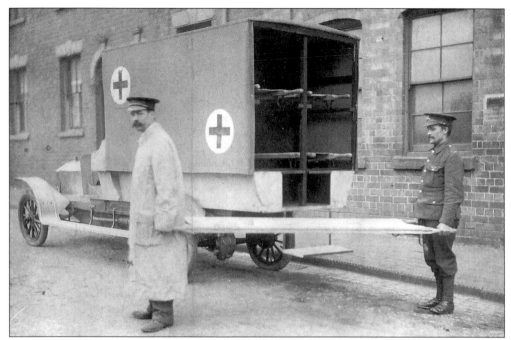

A Star ambulance outside the Briton Car factory in Stewart Street in 1916. The man on the right is Arthur Page of the Royal Army Medical Corps, who lived locally. He served on the Western Front (1915–1917) and was killed in action.

Aero-engine production in the Sunbeam factory in 1916. The engines are 150 hp V8 Crusaders, and 225 hp Mohawks. At the start of the war, Sunbeam was the only British manufacturer of high power aero-engines.

Sunbeam also built 647 aircraft during the First World War, including fifteen Short Bombers, one of which is shown here on Dunstall Park racecourse, which served as Wolverhampton's airfield. It is being tested with two bombs under each wing.

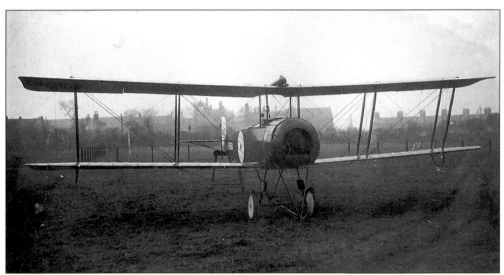

Sunbeam built 477 Avro 504 trainers, and this is one of the last ones to be built, though without its engine and propeller. It is seen on the Sunbeam recreation ground with the Royal Orphanage in the background.

A wartime Sunbeam float extolling the benefits of a female workforce. It is covered with Avro 504 parts. Sunbeam only built the fuselages of these aircraft, the wings being supplied by Star Engineering just down the road.

Sunbeam built the complete power cars for several airships. This one, ready for shipment to Cardington, was for the R.37 which was scrapped when ninety-five per cent complete.

The Sunbeam football team, 1918/19. They are seen with the BWAFA League Champions Cup, Wednesbury Charity Cup, Bass Cup, Lord Mayor of Birmingham's Cup and Turner & Simpson Charity Shield. On the back row, from left to right: W. Jackson, A. Brookes, B. Rostance, E. Collins, E. Clarke. On the middle row: L. Waddams, B. Jephson, F. Price, B. Creswell, R. Salter, W. Hawthorne, W. Flatley. On the front row: C. Palmer, W. Jennings, W. White, C.B. Kay (works' manager) A. Groves, J. Griffiths, S. Brookes, S. Read.

After the war car production returned to Sunbeam and this is the experimental shop, *c.* 1920.

Building the 1925 Sunbeam Grand Prix engine, a six cylinder, two litre, with twin OHC. They are, from left to right: Bill Timmins, Bill Murray, Alf Stokes, -?-, Jack Ridley.

The Royal Orphanage girl's hockey First XI, 1921. After the war, the orphanage was spared the sound of aero-engines being tested quite so often, but this was soon to be replaced by the sound of the Villiers' drop forge echoing around Blakenhall.

The welcome extended to Henry Segrave (with a bald head in the car) at the Moorfield Works after his historic victory for Sunbeam in the 1923 French Grand Prix.

St Luke's school football team, 1919/20. The headmaster, Robert Neville, is on the right.

Penn Road with the twin spires of St Paul's church, Blakenhall, in the distance in 1908.

St Paul's parish church on the Penn Road in 1936. It was built, in 1836, for the Revd William Dalton and was paid for by his wife, the wealthy widow of Richard Marsh of Lloyd House, so that he could move from Liverpool.

The 350 hp Sunbeam with a special Manitou aero-engine and three Sunbeam experimental shop fitters behind. They are, from left to right: Bill Murray, Tom Harrison, Mr Perkins. The car is outside the Sopwith Aircraft sheds at Brooklands in 1921.

The same car just afterwards, when it had crashed over the side of the Brooklands banking by the famous pilot, Harry Hawker. It was repaired and three years later became the first car in the world to exceed 150 mph, driven by Malcolm Campbell.

Malcolm Campbell sitting in a three litre Sunbeam outside the Moorfield Works canteen in 1926.

The '1,000 hp Sunbeam' being built in the Moorfield Works experimental department in 1927. Powered by two V12 OHC Matabele aero-engines, it became the first car in the world to exceed 200 mph.

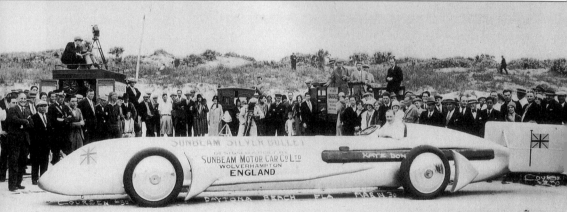

These two pictures were taken on almost the same spot on Daytona Beach, Florida. At the top can be seen Henry Segrave driving the 1000 hp Sunbeam which broke the world land speed record in 1927. At the bottom is Kaye Don driving the Sunbeam Silver Bullet in March 1930. It failed to beat the land speed record because of technical difficulties and weather conditions.

A celebration of Henry Segrave's record in the *Star & Garter*, Wolverhampton on 29 March 1927. Many of the workers who built the car are present and Segrave is the one with the towel behind his head. On his right is Mrs Segrave (the actress Doris Stocker) then to her right is Tommy Harrison, with Alec Broome looking over their shoulders. On Segrave's left is Jack Ridley then to his left is ? Perkins.

The Silver Bullet on display in America, with nose and tail painted red. It did break the American 5 km record.

The AJS motorbike production lines at Graiseley Hill in the 1920s.

AJS motorcycles awaiting packing and despatch at the Graiseley works.

AJS road testers outside the Graiseley Works. On the extreme left is Bill Huxtable (the chief tester) and on the extreme right is Hubert Millard (charge hand in charge of testing).

A group of AJS workers outside the Graiseley Factory probably in the 1920s.

An aerial view of the Villiers (foreground) and Sunbeam (background) factories in 1926. The Sunbeam sports ground can be seen to the rear.

Tom Whitlock, a Sunbeam road tester, sitting in the record breaking Sunbeam twelve cylinder which broke the Brooklands track record at 170 mph, with Kaye Don driving.

The Star gear box shop, in Frederick Street in 1927. As can be seen, finishing work required skilled use of the hand file.

Our new Telephone Nos. are :—
Wolverhampton 1666 & 1667
(also Private Exchange)

NEW OFFICES OF
THE VILLIERS ENGINEERING CO. LTD.
WOLVERHAMPTON

The new offices of Villiers Engineering on Marston Road. The company had been founded in 1898 by Charles Marston to provide cycle components for Sunbeamland and in 1913 had produced its first two-stroke engine.

H.S. 'Bert' Kershaw with the first Villiers engine-gear unit, the Mk.8D, in 1936. Bert came to be known as 'Mr Villiers'. He joined the development department in 1935 and rose to become chief tester, and was well known for his tours of Europe on Villiers-engined bikes.

TT bikes being prepared in the AJS racing department in the 1920s.

The AJS road testers outside the factory, ready to roar off down the Penn Road in the, new for 1927, Model H9s.

Boys and girls at the Royal Orphanage in 1939. By then the institution had expanded over the Penn Road with the purchase of Graseley Old Hall, where junior accommodation and playing fields were built.

The Royal Orphanage cricket team in 1936. On the back row, from left to right: Statham, Fellows, Hollis, Williams, Jones, Bett. On the middle row: Mr T.S. Harrsion, Brown, Field, Bond, Mr V.A. Sleath. On the front row: Price, Buckeridge.

The old windmill, built in 1750, was located in Mill Lane, near Chetwynd Road, off Villiers Street. Neither the mill nor the lane exist anymore.

Kirby's Nurseries in Haggar Street, Blakenhall *c.* 1932. They are, from left to right: Cyril, Margaret and Stanley Kirby; the latter two were twins. Haggar Street is behind them.

The Cottage, No. 1 Haggar Street, the home of Mr Kirby. His nursery was well known in the area, especially for the tomatoes he grew in his greenhouses.

Stanton's Bakery cart in the part of Moore Street which no longer exists. It is outside the house of Mr Gibbons, the photographer, who also sold lead soldiers and comics from the house. The first house, behind the cart, was that of Webley's, the bookmakers.

The wedding of Mr Darby and Rennee Davies from Sedgley Street, outside St Luke's church in 1934. They are from left to right: Joyce Davies, -?-, Mr Jones, Mr Darby, Renee Darby, Arthur Davies, -?-, Mildred Davies, and the little bridesmaid's name was ? Day.

The interior of St Luke's church in the 1930s, decorated either for the coronation or the Jubilee.

The Sunbeam closed in 1936 and one of the companies which took over the buildings was Fischer Bearings, a German concern. This is the grinding shop in 1937. The fifty or so German employees fled the country two days before war started and the company became British.

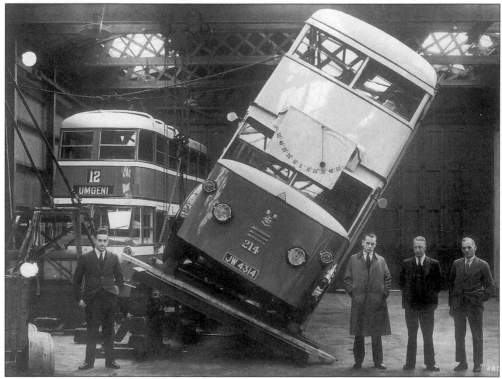

Sunbeam continued to make buses and this is a trolleybus under test in August 1934. Cyril Dabbs, the chief engineer is on the extreme left.

A Sunbeam bus chassis ready to be fitted with its bodywork outside the Moorfield Works. Contact Switchgear Ltd had occupied the building in the background by now.

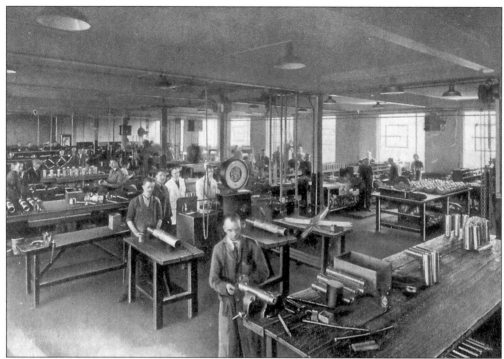

Another company to move into the Sunbeam buildings was Turner Engineering, which had once made steam cars and then petrol driven cars in Lever Street. While keeping the Lever Street factory they made aircraft undercarriages in the new Wulfruna Works, and here undercarriage legs for the Stirling bomber are being assembled.

Turner's fire department at the Wulfruna Works in 1944.

One of the major products at Villiers during the war was shell fuses (six million during the war), and like many wartime factories, women workers were employed in profusion, like these assembling the fuses.

Villiers 199 fuse shop employees in 1944. On the back row, from left to right: May Clark, Eadie Robinson, -?-, -?-, -?-, Lily Rounds, Lily Stewart, Dorothy Fryer, Lily Harrington. On the middle row : -?-, -?-, Lily Jones, Margaret ?, Maureen ?, -?-, Joan Wood, -?-, -?-, -?-,-?-, Elsie Thompson. The front row are all unknown.

The Royal Orphanage Cadet Corps during the war. The CO, Lt Col. C.R. Gibbs, who was also the headmaster, was awarded the MBE for services to the cadet movement in 1943.

An aerial view of the Royal School, as it has become, showing the new St Luke's school top right, and the new playing fields and junior accommodation in the grounds of Graseley Old Hall at the bottom.

Some of the staff at Turner's Lever Street factory in 1954. They are, from left to right: D. Pashmore, Mary Pandey, -?-, -?-, Phillip ?, Mary Rowland and (seated) Mrs Green. One of the things they made in Lever Street after the war, were rickshaws for China, so road vehicles were still being made in Blakenhall!

Brian Poulson, standing on Henry Gough's scaffolding on St Paul's church, c. 1951. His brother, Ernie, was involved in the restoration work and early in the morning would catch a sack full of pigeons as they emerged from their crevices. Brian then sold them for 1s 6d each from his loft. When they 'homed' back to the church, Ernie could catch them again. The spires of St John's and the Congregational church, Queen Street, are behind.

Inspecting engine components in the Villiers after the war. Though the company was mostly known for its engines, bicycle components like the freewheel remained major products.

Villiers apprentices under the supervision of W.A. 'Bill' Norton on the left in 1951. Bill Norton joined Villiers, in 1921, as a member of the engine experimental department, playing a large part in the development of the 175 cc Villiers Brooklands racing engine. He started the apprentice school in 1941 with four students and saw it expand to an annual intake of fifty by 1958.

The grinding shop in Fischer Bearings, or FBC as it was then usually known as part of the British Timken Group, in 1946.

A production of *Grand Hotel* given by Fischer Bearings' concert party in 1946. They are, from left to right: Gwen Porter, Leah Pritchard, Allen Vaughan. Leah Pritchard was said in the company magazine 'to have blossomed overnight into a first-rate comedienne'.

The visit of the Duke of Edinburgh to Fischer Bearings in 1948. The operator is Mrs W. Thompson on the assembly line, filling the inner and outer rings of the bearings with steel balls. She had worked at the company for over ten years, and had married the previous year.

Fischer Bearings employees wave goodbye to the Duke, and he turns to acknowledge their enthusiasm. He had of course recently married a glamorous princess.

The Fischer Bearings football team in 1950. On the back row, from left to right: Reynolds, Lee, Lee (captain), Springthorpe, Frisby, Carpenter, Hughes, Leach. On the front row: Leicester, Nicholls, Bowdler, Gibbs, Peplow, Briton, Lockley.

Wives and friends of Fischer Bearings employees on a visit to the factory in 1950.

St Luke's school in 1952. A new school has since been built on the former Sunbeam sports field.

A St Luke's year group in the playground, with the church behind, in 1953.

A party in the backyard of the Moss Rose pub in Moore Street, celebrating the coronation in 1953. They are, from left to right: Ted and Florrie Hodson, of Hall Street, Mr Hickman and Derek Hickman, Mr and Mrs Banks and their young son, the landlord's wife, her son, the landlord. The pub and that section of Moore Street and Hall Street have all been demolished to make way for Blakenhall Gardens.

The St Luke's school visit to Trentham Gardens in 1948. The children line up in the playground ready to board the coaches for a welcome relief from the rigours of wartime. In the war each child had been asked to bring a lump of coal to school each day and the one with the biggest lump sat nearest the fire.

All the Villiers apprentices, at a time when 2,100 people worked for the company, in 1958. Today there are just four in a spare parts operation.

The Scala cinema in Worcester Street served the inner end of Blakenhall. The cinema is still there, but has gone through a number of name changes as a night club.

The AJS factory building in Graiseley Hill just before it was demolished. A Safeway supermarket now occupies much of the site.

The 2,000,000th Villiers engine to be built, a 225 cc Mark 1H, is presented to C.F. Caunter (centre), assistant keeper of the Science Museum by H. Geoffrey Jones, managing director of Villiers.

The St Luke's girls' netball team in 1952.

The St Luke's boys' cricket team in 1952.

114

Enoch Powell, for many years the MP for Wolverhampton South West which included Penn and Blakenhall, on a visit to the Royal School in 1960.

The Old Royals (Royal School Old Boys) cricket team in 1960. The Old Royals Association for boys had been formed in 1929, and the Old Rowans for girls in 1932. On the back row, from left to right: K. Plant, J. Poutney, K. Hollingsworth, R. Poutney, T. Holt. On the front row: A. Calvert, R.W. Davies, R. Tilley, ? Gardner, ? Chattaway, D.B. Huffer.

The Queen Mother visiting the Royal School in 1960.

The Coliseum Cinema in Dudley Road, a suburban cinema with a longer life than most, having taken on the showing of Indian films in its latter years.

Graseley Old Hall in the late 1980s, just before it was bought by the actress Susan Williams and her brother who commenced its restoration. It became a listed building at the instigation of local MP, Enoch Powell.

A line up of Sunbeam cars at Bromley House which was built on the site of Louis Coatalen's residence. Coatalen was the chief engineer at the Sunbeam for most of its existence, and this occasion was the unveiling of a blue plaque by his granddaughter.

The 350 hp Sunbeam, the first of Malcolm Campbell's Blue Birds, on loan from the National Motor Museum for the opening of IMEX studios in the old Sunbeam experimental building. Peter Warren of IMEX is in Malcolm Campbell's seat.

Six
Graiseley

On the other side of the Penn Road from Blakenhall is the neighbouring suburb of Graiseley, which is very similar in character, with terraced houses clustered around factories, schools and churches. In fact only with the recent widening of the Penn Road has there been much of a distinction between the two areas. Before the physical barrier of the new dual carriageway, they were almost always regarded as one large suburb. The Stevens Brothers began building their engines in Pelham Street before moving to Retreat Street and then over the Penn Road to Graiseley House. Clyno then moved into their old Pelham Street works and Wearwell built the Wolf and Wulfruna ranges of motorcycles in Great Brickkiln Street. So Graiseley should share with Blakenhall the title of automotive capital of Great Britain, until all these famous companies folded around the Great Depression.

The children of Brickkiln Street school, opened on 25 March 1878 to replace Salop Street schools, were led in procession from their old school. It was a cold day, with snow falling, and afterwards they were given a bun each and a half day holiday. The tower no longer stands.

Clyno Engineering Company's staff outing in 1918; the motorbikes, which are all Clynos, were built a few yards away in Pelham Street. The building in the background is St Mark's school which still stands but is now the Wolverhampton United Services Club. Clyno moved from Northampton to be near their engine suppliers the Stevens Bros (AJS) of Retreat Street in 1909.

The inside of the Clyno factory and the first four ABC Dragonfly aero-engines being assembled in 1918. Clyno had an order for 500 Dragonflies, but had only completed about fifty when orders were cancelled in 1919; Clyno returned to motorbike and then car production.

Owen Road, Graiseley, in the 1920s. This was typical of the streets of terraced houses which filled the Graiseley area in Victorian times, many of which still stand today.

The staff of John Holmes Confectioners Ltd, Fern Road, Graiseley, *c*. 1925. In the centre are Tom Randle (manager) on the left, with Mrs Beatrice Randle to his right, and Mr Holmes, with Mrs Holmes to his left. Tom Randle has his hands on the shoulders of his son Walter.

Tom Green with one of the first milk lorries at Midland Counties Dairies, on the Penn Road. He retired for the first time in 1954 after forty-nine years, and for the third and last time in 1962, having picked up three gold watches for sixty-one years service!

Children from Cardiff, Lime, Bristol and Fisher Streets in Graiseley, c. 1947. They are about to go on their first outing after the war, to Sutton Park.

Four supporters of the Central Boys' Club at the top of Mander Street, outside the front door, *c.* 1951. They are, from left to right: Ted Nicholls (who owned a local timber firm), Colonel Burton (on the honorary staff), Field Marshall Auckinleck, Sir Charles Mander.

Bingley Street school football team, 1948/9. On the back row, from left to right: ? Widderson, Phil Parks, John Tipton, Don Yeats, -?-. On the front row: -?-, -?-, Don Tranter, Harry Howells, ? Woolly, ? Spruce.

Central Boys' Club boxing team, *c.* 1953. On the back row, from left to right: Ted Nicholls, -?-, -?-, Bill Edwards (PTI), Col. Bradbury. On the front row, the All National Champions: Jeff Turpin, Ron Davenport, Harry Hill, Terry MacKenzie, Malcolm Fellows.

The Central Boys' Club basketball squad, with PTI Bill Edwards on the right, *c.* 1948. They could not have realized that basketball is a non-contact sport as a couple of them are wearing boxing gloves!

Bingley Street juniors football team, Blakemore Cup winners, 1948/9. The air raid shelters are in the background to the right. At the rear is Mr Powell, then on the back row, from left to right: Dave Poyner, John Lees, Graham Leek, Peter Robinson, John Burton, Terry Lamsdale. On the front row: Terry Howell, Harry Murray, Brian Poulson (captain), Dickie Westley, Ray ?.

Bingley secondary modern school cricket team, 1950/1. On the back row, from left to right: Pete Higginson, ? Cocksall, Ron Green, Brian Poulson, -?-, -?-, -?-, ? Tomkys, Terry Lamsdal. On the front row: Pete Robinson, ? Brown, Mr Williams, Bryn Banks, Ray Cummins, Mr Swale, -?-, John Lees.

Brickkiln Street school nursery children, c. 1967.

Brickkiln Street boys' rounders team, c. 1970. On the back row, from left to right: Mr Kelso (headmaster) Brian Powney, A. Singh, ? Dodd, -?-, -?-, Mr B. Patel. On the front row, Lindsey Buckner, Campbell, -?-, -?-, -?-.

Bingley Street primary school teaching staff in 1977.

Acknowledgements

I could not have produced this book without the help and kindness of a large number of people, in particular Harry Blewitt for letting me once more borrow from his superb postcard collection, and Jim Boulton for his amazing private archive of local history.

I am very grateful to Mike Williams, editor of the *Wolverhampton Chronicle*, for letting me seek photographs through the medium of the Memory Lane page. Without that help I would not have come across many of the following people.

Among the others I have to thank are, and I apologize if I have forgotten anyone:
Mr D. Armstrong, Mrs J. Cockfield, Bill Edwards, Bob Edwards, Ray Edwards, Harry Evans, Mrs Fletcher, B. and W.F. Fowler, Gerald Gabb, Mr Haddock, Mr Hastings of Brickkiln primary school, Mr J. Hill, Mr Ray Jones, Mary Keay-Harris, Percy Kyte, Ron Le Doux of Penn Hall school, Mr K. Millard, Penn golf club, John Peplow of the Penn cricket club, Ken Peplow, Gwen Porter, Brian Poulson, Mrs Price, Ann Rigby of Perth WA, Mr C. Robinson, The Royal School, Mary Simmonds of NSW, Mrs M. Smith, St Bartholmew's school, St Luke's school, Kevin Summers, John Tipton, Walter Turner, Mr Turvey, Frank Wedge, Mrs R.Wilcox, Basil Wilding, Susan Williams of Graseley Old Hall, Mr K. Winslow, Mrs Wooldridge, and always last but never least Wendy Matthiason.